Light
Before the Sun

Light Before the Sun

poems

Sister Sharon Hunter, CJ

PARACLETE PRESS
BREWSTER, MASSACHUSETTS

2026 First Printing

Light Before the Sun: Poems

ISBN 979-8-89348-038-2

Library of Congress Cataloging-in-Publication Data

Names: Hunter, CJ, Sharon, 1947- author.
Title: Light before the sun : poems / Sharon Hunter, CJ.
Description: Orleans : Paraclete Press, 2025. | Summary: "These meditations reflect on the light the author discovered in the challenges and experiences encountered in her life, as she shares her vulnerable and redemptive journey"-- Provided by publisher.
Identifiers: LCCN 2025038757 (print) | LCCN 2025038758 (ebook) | ISBN 9798893480382 (trade paperback) | ISBN 9798893480399 (epub)
Subjects: BISAC: | POETRY / Subjects & Themes / Inspirational & Religious
Classification: LCC PS3608.U594964 L54 2025 (print) | LCC PS3608.U594964 (ebook)
LC record available at https://lccn.loc.gov/2025038757
LC ebook record available at https://lccn.loc.gov/2025038758

10 9 8 7 6 5 4 3 2 1

Published by Paraclete Press
Brewster, Massachusetts
www.paracletepress.com

Printed in the United States of America

CONTENTS

I
Complexities of Light

II
Fundamental Seasons

III
Calculated Turbulence

IV
Tunneling Light

V
Rough Places Plain

VI
Simple Fare

VII
Light Frequency

Epilogue

I

Complexities of Light

Wavefront

Life is a stained-glass window:
the intricate colors
patterns of experience.

One hopes their window
is infused with joy.
But opaque places
challenge light
that begs admittance.

Lost in remembrance,
I trace the patterns
on the window of my soul . . .
counting interlocking colors.

The Great Watcher

I dreamt of a snow leopard.
The beautiful creature
appeared improbably
on my porch.
Its massive paws
and piercing eyes
piqued my interest.

That's the way of dreams.
They jolt us
from the ordinary,
open our minds
to the exiled realms
our hearts refuse
in waking hours.

Some call the snow leopard
The Great Watcher.
It's fiercely protective,
primal,
and irreplicable.
A visible promise of transformation.

On waking,
porch empty once again,
I pounced upon those exiled realms.
A framed picture
of a snow leopard
now sits on my desk,
urging me to dream.

To Be Alone

It's our nature
to admire the good,
walk beside the strong,
and leave uncertain unchallenged.
But who are we?

I've dark places to go,
where "almost" isn't good enough,
and I won't be held captive
by the vagaries of alone.

Fear.

Closed spaces,
the entrance lost.
A relationship that controls:
a beginning without an end,
and a persistent
failed attempt
to swallow.

No way back.
No way out.
No way home.
In summation: Isolation.

The Source

This silent invader
shows no mercy
. . .
observes
no
boundaries.

What is its source,
this clever parasite
embedded in our DNA?

Sadness.

A song unsung.
A bell unrung.
Forgotten dreams
remain unfound.
So near a smile
that isn't given.
A warmth
held back.
A poem unwritten.

Blackberry Summer

On a clear summer day,
grandfather promised
to go berry picking with his girls.
As they waited,
as the wind made leaves
dance at mother's feet,
he lay dead in a coal shaft.

"An accident," some said.
Others, "murder."
Two little orphans
forever question,
"When is Papa coming home?"

And I,
decades later,
amongst the muffled silence
of airless rooms
and their unexplained noises,
race without a finish line.

Worth a Thousand Words

Karl found a photograph,
and thought it should be mine.
"A picture of your dad."
I'm wary.
I want to refuse.
Why reignite the reconciled?
But distant family,
does the proper thing.
It arrived in the mail,
fresh from the attic,
packed with good intentions,
and splintered shards of memory.

So father eyes me
from my mother's bureau.
Expecting guests,
the lady herself
stands at the mirror.
Revlon and Maybelline
mystically transform her
between sips of scotch and soda.
"Nice picture," I said,
pleased it'd found a home.

Mother smirked.
"Drunk as a skunk."
I looked again.
Reality curled its finger
my direction.

Weightless

Scarred moments.
Destroyed hopes.
Blunt words,
deplete the air
of joy,
of consolation.

I leave the moment.
Mother's newfound beauty
unbeautifully ignored.
Memories,
for all their shining moments
can't change the flow
of time.

Night, Phase Two

A car tops the hill
of our driveway,
stops a safe distance
from the porch
where our spaniel lies
on a bed of blankets.

I run to an open window.
Eight years old,
hands white on the frame,
I observe my father,
slouched against the car,
brushing her shoulder,
regaling my brother's fiancée
with alcohol-laced anecdotes.

He passes me
— Brian —
hurt and angry
on the stairway.
Though a child,
I embody sanity:
the active listener.
"He's out there
slobbering all over her!"

I feel an inward crush of shame.
I sorrow for my brother,

sorrow for Kathy,
but most of all,
for my father.
He wears disgrace
as if it's deserved.
Our outfits
and motivations match.
At eight years old,
unable to coax him inside,
I stand clothed
in the supposition
that I'm the one to blame.

II

Fundamental Seasons

Immutable Love

Love can build,
create,
shield
and emancipate.

Love's a gift that knows no price,
and yet is still a thing that's prized.
Rarely offered,
seldom viewed
and hardly ever recognized.

Love's Adversary

Hate is held back,
by clever disguises.
It lurks in silence,
sulks in shadow,
searching
for fertile grounds
fragile places
to feast, unrepentant.

Hate ingests the good,
leaving behind bones,
desolation and rubble:
the remnants of life
that forgot to bend.

Out of Context

I'll blame you
just for a while,
as memories need sifting through:
tenebrous memories
in need of illumination
before they're healed.

Once bleak and overpowering,
a power wash of copium
reduces them to remnants:
pocket-sized good intentions;
poorly conceptualized relationships.

Immaculate stairs
built in the wrong place,
guide me
toward a colossal,
mutually destructive
mistake.

Fish on the Line

When you're young,
you believe
in love sought
and love found.

Somehow, you know:
they looked at you
because of something special
in your quietness,
something worthy of notice,
never mind the source.

But the shadow above water
gives no thought
to the small,
complicated
creature below.
Looking not to love,
but for easy game:
a fish on the line
for lean times.

Walk gently, careless angler!
Your unsuspecting prey,
with their exhaustless need
for acceptance and assurance,
may not stay on ice!

Keep searching
for the right fish:
grateful for the tether,
comfortable in captivity.

When found,
some reel it in,
and toss it back,
satisfied.

Still others,
line secure,
— smug and confident —
slowly prepare the net.
But haven't you heard?
Fishing
is two-way
deception.

Circular Journey

The wedding was small,
just the necessary elements:
bride, groom,
family, friends,
and a stranger in a black shirt
with a white collar
asking required questions.
Beauty. Simplicity.
In that, I had my way.
Tasteful dresses,
flowers with just enough ribbon,
and a gracious sampling of food,
all color-matched,
appropriate
and all marred
by the groom's
small victory:
liquor at the reception.
Having lost that battle,
I gave my first married moments
to incessant worry
over soon-to-come embarrassment.
Time is a loop of experiences,
and history a mirror of our actions.
Nothing past has passed.

The wedding dissolves
into the marriage,
and we wait
for happily ever after.

Love of Attrition

I search for mislaid individuality
among his misadventures,
while his mind
lingers at the bar
or somewhere else
far from me.

I married to escape chaos
and emotional infidelity,
but like the locks on our mobile home,
the broken endured.
I realized,
barricaded in the bedroom,
promises abandoned,
that I'd married my history.

A Hand Overplayed

The game is well played,
but you underestimate
the depth of my will,
my ferocious need to survive.

Push me, shake me, insult me,
alienate me from those I love . . .
I'll stick around for more.
I'm comfortable with pain.

But do not lock me away,
ignored, untouched and unheard.
In sealing that box,
you've ensured my liberation.

III

Calculated Turbulence

Defeated and Depleted

On a sunny Friday,
I rode to hell
in a Ford Mustang.
"Pack a bag," he said.
I was going to the hospital.
Silly me,
I pictured a quiet room
and a worry-free week
of kindness, care, and safety.

I was twenty-three
and precariously outmatched.
His eyes saw only
the dark underside
of my mountain.
Dependent and desperate,
I settled for the role
of insignificant other.

My head rested on my hand,
and my hand on the car window.
There was to be an exchange:
my leafy-green summer dress
for pallid, hospital green walls.
A hostage in all but name.

No Turning Back

The door closes,
heavy and immutable.
I'm lost in a maze
of small rooms,
corridors, and strangers
with empty eyes
and soundless voices.

Judge them?
No, I fear them,
fear it's contagious,
or worse, inevitable.
I'm aware I have a choice
and must refuse an easy out.

He turns and leaves,
and I watch him
to see if he looks back.
He doesn't.
He walks without shame,
or remorse.
For once, he's satisfied.
He goes for a stroll,
the pole still in the water.
That fish ain't going nowhere.

Sometimes

I want to be nobody.
Can I be nobody?
Just a quiet thought
taking up little space.

Let me be gentle.
Let me be wise.
Let me be silent.
Let me be aware.

If I removed in myself
all but those things,
I'd be left with nothing,
and that's just fine by me.

Truth or Consequences

The nurse thinks I slept well
and enjoyed breakfast.
Why?
Because I told her so.
Already, I've deserted truth
in favor of escape.
She smiles,
declaring me
the ideal patient.

But I'm still watched
as the key is turned,
and the blank button pressed.
Still watched as gears jolt into action.
With two sturdy men in white
I descend via elevator
to the unlabeled lobby
to meet my assigned psychiatrist.

He's neither impressed nor intrigued.
I am a simple stop on his hurried journey.
One glance before prescriptions are scribbled.
Really? That's it?
But I have so many secrets to tell.
"Next time," he promises.

Observe and Calculate

I pass a room
where leather restraints
decorate the walls.
In that ill-famed room,
they shock sense into people.
As best I can,
I avoid contact
with folks in white.

I join a group in the elevator.
Going up, a woman cries out,
telling the air that she should be happy:
she has everything she's ever wanted
and still wants to kill herself.
I stay silent.
Invisible.

After lunch, promised medications arrive.
Before, my mind raced in pursuit of clarity.
But I'm the new model.
The medicated version.
In me, a thought troupe
of gypsy acrobats
tumbles freely,
uninhibited by concerns
of when
          and where
                    to land.

Doubt Pollution

Doubt slipped under the door,
unwelcomed and uninvited.
It snaked its way
from my past
to my now
and my future.

So hard to discern,
so difficult to discourage.
Doubt knows how to distort,
and disparage reality.

Here. Take my truth.
Twist it into *your* version.
Play make believe
while you can.
The cycle
inevitably
circles back.
Three-point doctrine
learned the hard way:
read between lines,
examine fine print,
trust, but verify.

All in Favor

I'm to visit home.
It's a test really,
its overseer the very man
who discarded me.
He'll evaluate my qualifications
for good old American wifehood.
Would it be a quick release or a longer stay?
So much for impartiality.

My spouse arrives,
a flurry of self-importance.
He walks past me
to greet the staff,
as an accomplished equal:
social worker and mentor
to drug-addicted delinquents
like himself.

Sympathetic looks are exchanged.
"A shame about HER."
Rigorous nodding
sends my husband's shoulder-length hair
bobbing up down his grown-up suit.
And then the arrow,
sharp and precise.
We're to visit his family,
instead of mine.

He has a case to prove:
devoted husband presents
problem wife to self-deluded parents.
Quite the headline.
All the better
to divorce you with,
my dear!

In the car, he's Mr. Big Shot.
I deflect his oozing superiority.
He doesn't know it yet,
but he's already lost.
I have the upper hand
and will never yield
to his monstrous betrayal.
I sense another presence in the car:
Guilt.
Guilt is an unrelenting companion.

Light Intrusion

I shake off lethargy,
ignoring the voices
that ambush my mind.
I'm ready.
I'm informed
and experientially wise.
"A smart aleck on pills,"
according to my husband.
The pill part is wrong.
I stopped taking them days ago.

He senses I'm gaining confidence,
and reminds me I'm useless.
Return to captivity
is but a finger snap away.
No longer am I cowed by his opinion.
I will not relinquish my autonomy
for overmedicated hell.
Not now, not ever.

He Said, She Considered

I was the one who would never,
courage free in danger, forever.
Who couldn't, who wouldn't.
Had no common sense.
I see, I see. And I agree.
Immediately,
sans suspense . . .
yet family holds
collective breath
for slipping sanity
isolation and death.
Someone must surrender
even if circumstantially,
and I volunteer.

IV

Tunneling Light

The Reset Button

Seven hundred miles away,
I get a new job,
and new friends.
Burdened by
the grief of failure,
I push onward.
Shy and wordless,
I force-feed myself life
even as my thin frame
becomes thinner.

I mumble demands
to people I push away.
I wait,
but not from patience.
I pray,
but not from belief.
I've simply no alternative.
I swallow pride.
I swallow hurt.
I swallow indignation.
Mostly, I demand resolution.

In the Valley of Baca

Love is light.
Mine?
It's in a glass jar
waiting for release.
I clasp the jar.
It's safely capped.
Preserved for another time.

But suddenly, I'm terrified.
Will it dissipate unopened?
If forgotten, evaporate?
If evaporated, replaced?

Light is hard to capture,
so I keep mine in a glass jar,
carrying it always,
for the bruised
and needy . . .
like me.

Cheat Me Twice, Shame on Me

To secure a divorce, one needs proper advice:

Psychological. "Go out and find someone who truly loves you."
The doctor says I'm of sound mind.
Sure, but my self-confidence is nonexistent.

Legal. "So the real problem is booze and broads."
Well spoke, kind sir. I'm a fan of brutal reality.
I've found the right lawyer.

Spiritual. "Don't seek divorce, nor resist it."
That one's tough to chew.
My sweet retaliation, denied.

Silver Linings

Christmas Eve, 1973,
I receive a registered letter,
signature required.
Divorce papers,
signed, sealed, and delivered.
Really?
After all this time
he chose Christmas?

I view it through two prisms:
A cruel action by a selfish man
perfectly timed for maximum hurt.
Or . . .
a Christmas gift from God:
final release from what was
that should never have been.

When Life Leads

I chose the road, and the road chose me.
I hope it's where I'm meant to be.
The path is neither high nor low,
it's just a place I need to go.
I yield my pride for an empty shell.
Dignity – my fused-on crown.
I yield my pride and yield it well.
The world I knew – tossed upside down.

Running on Empty

Words nest inside me,
unexpressed,
a confused mixture
of wickedness
and good intentions.

My help is misshapen,
unwelcome and misunderstood.
I fear nothing so much
as self-made chaos
and controversy.
I knock
on the door
of invisibility.
I beg entry,
imploring the walls
to swallow me
and hide me
in their neutrality.
To observe life,
without joining in

When Love Says "No"

God withdraws without stated reason,
surrenders me to self-exploration.
Unfit to be a weigher of souls,
I know not how to judge my own.
My judgement is harsh.
I lean into negativity,
like a dear lost friend.
Positivity leads to disappointment,
disillusionment and unbelief.
It's better to remain
slightly beneath it all.
Thick skin
over thicker skin . . .
over thicker skin.

Living Without

My heart transports blood
to the needed places,
but it's stopped growing.
There is no heart to my heart,
just the robotic beating
that keeps me alive.

My love has stagnated.
If those who claim love
prove unfaithful,
how do you forgive?
"Words," piped a little bird.
"Cheep, cheep, cheap."

Upon Reflection

Loneliness, my truest friend,
escort me into nothingness.
Nothing to lose;
nothing to gain.
Just empty space:
a jelly doughnut
lacking the filling
that gives it its name.
I consider forgiveness and redemption
as I search for a higher purpose:
hope and love beyond myself,
and shelter in the hands of God . . .
but all the while, He remains silent.

V

Rough Places Plain

Standing on the Edge

The rhythmic essence of life
is interwoven with words
that dance on the airwaves.
Their passing magic reverberates,
rejuvenating and reviving
those who wait in poignant expectation.

The cliff's sharp edge
no longer tempts me
with its abrupt ending.
This chapter is essential;
it's part of the journey,
part of the search.
When my book has ended,
I shall know I travelled well.
I walked beside, and never alone.

So Let It Be

To love more than we're loved,
to answer the calling to do so,
we must accept that love
isn't ours to have nor render.
It's a gift without thought of return:
the essence of One who loves
more than He is loved,
who deserves more than we
who stand perplexed and wait,
pondering the lack of reciprocity.

So why do these hands
ineptly grasp at hollowness?
Why do I ignore the love
that lies bleeding at my feet?
He suffered for the likes of me,
yet I, too stubborn,
self-absorbed, and rigid,
refuse to stoop and touch
fragile holiness
that radiates
redemption.

Right, Left, Right

Life for me is a child's game of hopscotch,
bouncing from one wrong foot to the next.
Hop, hop, trip.
Jump, hop, fall.
Up again,
back again,
down again,
try again.

My heart cries peace.
My mind a spinning top:
whirling and twirling.
atop the chalk lines.
Up again,
back again,
down again,
try again.

One of Each

How can I be what I cannot?
God created equal but not identical.
I fight the sensor which insists
my differences are an abomination.
Your sense of belonging
fails to comfort me.
Your self-confidence
cannot be emulated
by an addled mind.

Every soul is made in His image,
each true to the sequence God initiated:
limitless diamonds reflecting the sun
and its multifaceted brilliance.
Equal does not mean the same.

The Gleaning Field

I am Ruth in the gleaning field,
gathering life from its surplus yield,
offered me by my Savior kind,
left to me as a sacred sign.

The fruit of suffering, fruit of hope;
the savior's love a lifeline rope.
I gather barley, gather wheat
to place them at the Savior's feet.

In holy ground devoid of whim,
I pluck the root of Jesse's stem.
All things start and all things end;
all things bow and all things bend.

I'm not alone in gleaning field,
I have a guide with silver shield,
cloak of virtue and arrows gold.
I am a sheep of the Master's fold.

Hireling

Build.
What shall I build?
An altar to the Lord.
Of what shall I build it?
Bricks from straw.
Where is the straw?
Within.

All I have is mud and straw.
I am not strong.
I am not pure.
I am not worthy.
Am I brave?
No.
Willing?
No.
What then is left?
Beauty from sin confessed.
Life from sin forgiven.
Mud and straw,
forged strong as steel.

Maybe One Day

As better Christians pray,
my inadequate thoughts,
pitiful winds of illusion,
are my prayer "contributions."
Oh God, help me to learn
not to tell you what to do
or suggest how to do it,
but to speak your words,
words from the Holy Spirit,
not idle talk to fill the void.

Unamazing Me

I shout when I want to cry.
Run when I should hold fast,
confused by my own confusion.
Yet, somewhere is a settling place
where I can breathe and know
in the words of the saint,
that all shall be well.

Prayers of the Hypocritical

I demand justice,
condemn evildoers
and plead for others
that they repent.
And all the while,
I am they.
I lie and exaggerate.
I disregard the rights of friends.
I tread on the weak,
preying on their weaknesses.
Jesus ordered me
from the synagogue.
I've often wondered
who *they* were.
Now I know.

Moment to Moment

And of the twelve,
where sits the traitor?
Surely it's not I, Rabbi?
I ask, with a darkened heart,
blistered by the sun of desire.
Resistant to the pleadings of your Love,
I go on pursuing existential pleasures:
temporary solace
that each day
leaves me emptier
than the last.

VI
Simple Fare

Re-Birth Fanfare

The broody hen has left her nest.
So little birds then break their shells,
puff out tiny yellow chests,
their wings aflutter as wind swells.

Fuzzy heads bathed in warm light.
Tiny feet embracing straw,
they know naught of flight or strife.
Newly hatched,
missing mom,
they're summoned
right to life.

Jump.

Jump over.
Land softly.
Touch lightly.

Rise to the occasion.
Smile at the wind.
Break out the sunshine.
Share a cup of trust.

Not you?
Then who?
Don't you know
that someone must?

From the Mouths of Babes

The wood fire sparked and crackled,
lifted its flame-arms to receive
marshmallows on sticks
attached to little hands.
My brother who was three years old,
and not prone to long exhortations,
whispered in the glowing silence:
"The parkz look like the tarz up in the ky."
That pesky old "s,"
too tough to master,
ignited kind laughter.
Years later, the story retold,
I paused mid-laugh to consider
the brilliant observation and connection.
A bit of heaven drew close to earth
and touched the heart of a little boy:
an up-close encounter
with the Living Creator
of all things.

Rollin' Like a River

This story is recounted
at family gatherings
filled with reminiscence,
but it's sometimes forgotten
that my brother and I are alike.
I shared his proclivity
for avoiding the dreaded "s."

Linda, my younger sister,
more joyful by nature,
more fun-loving than I,
invited me for a rolling-race
down our yard's steep hill.
This was a daunting feat
requiring us to lie stiff,
our bodies stretched taut.

No Push Offs Allowed.

I eyed the sun and lush green grass,
then weighed my chances of winning.
"Well, okay," I relented,
before issuing a dire warning:
"Just watch out for thithles and dog thit."
Indeed.

Back to Our Future

After mother was orphaned
she was raised on a farm
by her grandmother
and other relatives.
They loved her,
but worked her hard:

their myriad rules of conduct
were unbefitting a spunky child.
At the age of eighteen
a horse and buggy arrived
holding a handsome Scotsman.

When he came calling, Mother answered.
With empty pockets and little ado,
their wedding was fueled on love.
With a smile, she bid farewell
to home, kin and rules of conduct.
She was headed for the big city
There they danced the Charleston,
smoked like chimneys
with fireplaces lit by eternal flame,
drank like Prohibition was over . . .
and in more ways than one, it was.

When Mom Got Guilty

We were five children
in a three-story farmhouse,
so, in our early lives
religious training
was oft neglected.
But just in time, Mother's
pious upbringing roared in:
a guilt-filled freight train
on a collision course
with the Hunter children.

Thelma Jenkins, our religious neighbor,
was pianist at Highland Avenue Methodist.
Her attendance matched the church calendar;
mom didn't hesitate to enlist her aid.
Shy and introverted,
I dreaded interacting
with proper church members
forced to welcome me to the fold.

One memorable Easter Weekend,
Mom's guilt reached Richter frequencies.
She called Thelma, arranged transportation,
and informed her brood of her plans.
But there were unforeseen complications.
The first, and greatest of which:
our lack of appropriate clothing.

Our closet yielded no frilly dresses,
its wares devoid of beribboned hats,
gloves or patent leather Mary Janes.
I cautiously mentioned the situation,
hoping to quash the church escapade,
and return to sandbox tunnel building.
No such luck.

Mom, a perambulating stick of tobacco-scented incense,
sped off in our '56 pick-up to McFarland's General Store.
A short time later, a few dollars poorer,
she returned triumphantly clutching,
in lieu of any new church outfits,
a half-dozen boxes of Rit Dye
and token candy bars to buy us off.

She gathered her troops for instructions.
My oldest sister was stationed in the yard
surrounded by dye and metal wash tubs
as mother manned the garden hose.
The tubs soon swirled with various blues,
stirred about wildly with wooden spoons.
We'd reached the point of no return.
Doubt remained caught in my throat
as well-worn school dresses,
fresh from their hangers,
hit the dye.

Under mother's watchful eye,
we took turns "churning" the dresses,
leaving no area untouched.
The dresses were transformed
from their original dull colors
to erratic multi-shades of blue.
Line drying didn't save them.
We didn't stand a chance
in anyone's Easter Parade.
Undaunted, Mom smiled, satisfied.

Come next morning,
I climbed into Thelma's car,
soon to be stuck in the middle
of respectable Church members
who wouldn't remember my name,
but sure as the hell they sought to avoid
would remember that dress.

Musical Reveries

John Denver is a poet
with a guitar in hand.
He left behind
a trove of memories
set to melodies:
intricate,
profound
accessible.

There's wisdom in his words,
substance in his contemplation.
Exceptional integrity,
tie-dyed fabric,
fine-edged
in musical notation.
What is its origin, its source?
After all, he's just a "country boy,"
for which he gratefully thanks God.

Cabin Fever

"A tick and a tock," said the mantle clock.
"A chirp and a peep," said the crickets that creep.
"A doodle, doodle, doo," crowed the fine feathered rooster.
A creak then a squeak from the wind-swayed timber . . .
oh, the sounds in a one-roomed house
early morn on a sleepless night.

VII

Light Frequency

Come Dance with Me

My Lord, who loves me,
stops my flight.
His hand outstretched.
His eyes alight.
"Come dance with Me," says He.
He with smile so bright.
But rather than agree,
I fight.
"I've two left feet."

I backed away
remote and masked,
and wished
my Savior
hadn't asked.
The music played
and all but me
joined angelic melody.

But I've two left feet!
How can I dance
with two left feet?
How can I join
a song so sweet?
But even though I tried to hide
I heard the words of my gentle guide:
"Come dance with Me."

It was then
I took His hand
and bravely tried.

The Search for Meaning

I'm renowned for proficiency,
possessor of small gifts,
sifted by large goals . . .
irrespective of my purpose.

The Stuff of Stars

Words fall from the sky like stars
and I've but a moment to catch them,
to deftly connect them
in the jigsaw puzzle
of my mind.

Floating Thoughts

Thoughts drifted on the lazy stream of summer.
I reached out to capture a few,
enticing them to coalesce
and yield their beauty . . .
but the door opened
to irresistible diversion.

What happened to that lovely thought?
Pen hovers uselessly over paper.
It was something about the wind.

But the thoughts themselves
are particles too small
to resist being blown about
by the fancies of the breeze.

Follow the Wind

From my window,
I watch the wind pass by
as I listen to its music.

Winter bare branches,
sway and dance like actors
frolicking on life's stage.
But what story do they tell
as they bounce on their toes
or bend in silent obeisance?

I am the wind on a windy day.
From huffs and puffs
my gusts of bluster
buffet fellow man.
I drown the verbally downed in apology,
but "Go away" is what I'm hoping.
Leave me to my musings
while I gather strength
for yet another day.

Hear Its Roar

Outside, a dog barks.
And barks.
Little though he is,
wind compels him
to rid the world of danger.
What invisible enemies
does your noise disperse?
I'm snug and warm
behind my window.
We're better now,
the wind and me.
It travels on,
sweeping the earth,
shifting the old
to use as mulch
for the new day.

In My Father's House

You have a room for me,
though born without a room.
You've prepared a place for me,
though yourself displaced.

Tell me of my room.
I need to know.
You created beauty
and all things beautiful,
so how special it must be.
Are the walls painted white,
and covered in colorful art:
flowers and starry skies,
birds alight on leafy branch?

Is there a corner for quietness?
Allowance for needs unhealed?
A pruning place for unrequited sins?
Will I be alone as I oft prefer?
Can I watch the playoffs?
Oh! Could I have a dog?
A small one preferably.
And a backyard
with a rose garden.
In my room,
so thoughtfully prepared,
shall I know joy at last?

My Shepherd

I hear you in the song of winter wind
that carries with it hints of finest snow.
When I'm alone and lonely in that space
I feel the silence like an undertow
that pulls my heart to shadowy abyss,
for in your absence, hope does not exist.

Yet still my shepherd calls in gentle voice
to leave behind all cunning and all schemes.
He promises to make all hearts rejoice,
and calm the many agitated streams.
Feelings warped by life's suspected whim,
on rocky face I cling, then walk with Him.

Without Measure

The deep murrrr
of a mama cow
is answered
by the gentle lowing
of her smalling calf.
All is quiet and rustic,
filled with Holy Love.
There is light from a star
and the lingering sound
of blended angel voices.
At the manger's heart
lies both shepherd and lamb,
Jesus, wrapped in swaddling clothes
of purest simplicity.
And from his infant eyes a gaze
embraces all mankind.

A Slender Thread

I walk a path in pilgrim's search
of life beyond the seen and known.
I leave behind all that impedes.
Without companion, tread alone.

A slender thread still holds me fast,
sylph-like, yet as strong as steel.
At its furthest end there waits
the keeper of my path and keel.

Hold up, now.
Let me rest 'neath sun's soft beams.
Prepare my bed on restless leaves.
Soothe the coldness of my heart
with the warmth of ancient breeze.

Then I'll rise for journey's end,
for the thread still guides me true.
Through foggy day and murky night,
I'll stay the Pilgrim's path to You.

Divine Rhapsody

We are one at last,
The Lord and I,
no longer in a war
of fearsome words.
I am His and He is mine,
I, the recipient,
He, the giver
of infinite compassion.

Epilogue

Pearl of Great Price

They say it is hidden here
along the Pilgrim trail,
its hiding place shifting
based on its seeker's soul.

Come, let's search together.
We'll walk the streets,
extend the beggar's coin,
offer tonic to the sick,
catch those about to fall.

Is it found in the practical:
the mowing of grass,
the washing of dishes?
Or is it visible in a sunset
while the night stars
await their debut?

Perhaps, I ponder,
my pearl is found
in absence.
The absence of fear,
absence of doubt,
absence of the bruised ego
obscuring my vision.

Things important
mere steps ago

have lost significance.
God is at his work
shaping our clay.
And the treasure
for which I search?
The nearby pearl,
though still elusive,
is within my reach.

ACKNOWLEDGMENTS

Light Before the Sun was edited by Mitchell Bogatz, Managing Editor of Mitchell Bogatz Editing Services, Goleta, California. His knowledge, life experience, and compassion combined to lift my humble word-offerings above themselves. With gratitude . . .

Author, screenwriter, editor, and teacher, he can be contacted by email at Mitchellbogatz.com.

ABOUT THE AUTHOR

This is the book I would not have written. These are the words best left unspoken, the memories left unopened. This is the book of pain long avoided, mistakes underestimated, healing light unshed on wounds of unreality. Each time I turned my back, rebuffed a friend, refused the pen, I further entrenched myself in a life without purpose. Until to fully live, I no longer had an option; I found myself tethered to my own conviction that light comes before the sun's warm glow.

To quote from "Standing on the Edge":

The rhythmic essence of life
is interwoven with words
that dance on airwaves.
Their passing magic reverberates,
rejuvenating and reviving
those who wait in poignant expectation.

This chapter is essential; it's part of the journey, part of the search. When the book has ended, I shall know I travelled well. I walked beside, and never alone.

ABOUT PARACLETE PRESS

Paraclete Press is the publishing arm of the Cape Cod Benedictine community, the Community of Jesus. Presenting a full expression of Christian belief and practice, we reflect the ecumenical charism of the Community and its dedication to sacred music, the fine arts, and the written word.

www.paracletepress.com

"O that my words were written down!
O that they were inscribed in a book!
O that with an iron pen and with lead
they were engraved on a rock forever!"
—Job 19:23–24

Outcast and utterly alone, Job pours out his anguish to his Maker. From the depths of his pain, he reveals a trust in God's goodness that is stronger than his despair, giving humanity some of the most beautiful and poetic verses of all time. Paraclete's Iron Pen imprint is inspired by this spirit of unvarnished honesty and tenacious hope.

OTHER IRON PEN BOOKS

Almost Entirely, Jennifer Wallace
Andalusian Hours, Angela Alaimo O'Donnell
Begin with a Question, Marjorie Maddox
The Consequence of Moonlight, Sofia Starnes
Cornered by the Dark, Harold J. Recinos
Eye of the Beholder, Luci Shaw
Exploring This Terrain, Margaret B. Ingraham
From Shade to Shine, Jill Pelaez Baumgaertner
Glory in the Margins, Nikki Grimes
Idiot Psalms, Scott Cairns
Iona, Kenneth Steven
Litany of Flights, Laura Reece Hogan
Raising the Sparks, Jennifer Wallace
There Is a Future, Amy Bornman
To Shatter Glass, Sister Sharon Hunter, CJ
Wing Over Wing, Julie Cadwallader Staub

YOU MAY ALSO BE INTERESTED IN

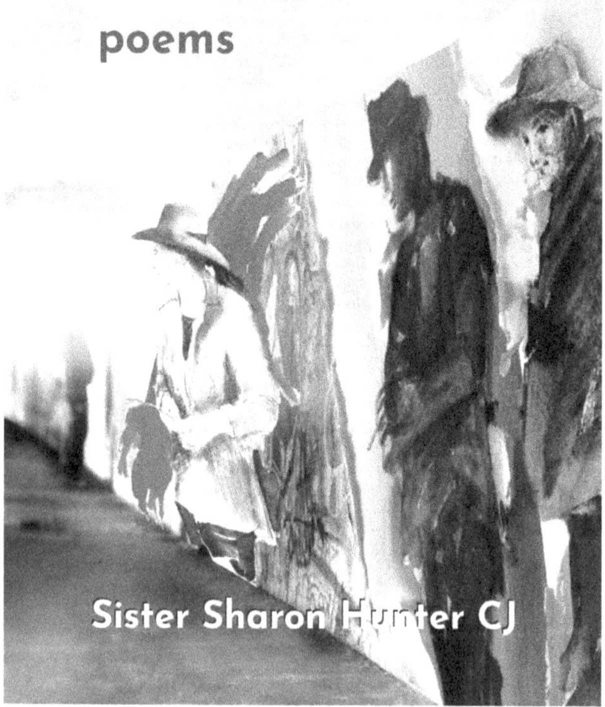
CHANCE
ENCOUNTERS
poems
Sister Sharon Hunter CJ